SPOT

A GIFT FOR:

_____

FROM:

_____

DATE:

_____

Crazy About My Dog

BARBOUR
PUBLISHING

CRAZY ABOUT MY DOG™

COPYRIGHT © 2003 BY MARK GILROY COMMUNICATIONS, INC.
TULSA, OKLAHOMA

ART AND DESIGN BY JACKSONDESIGNCO, llc
SILOAM SPRINGS, ARKANSAS

ISBN 1-58660-856-8

SCRIPTURE TAKEN FROM FROM *THE MESSAGE*.
COPYRIGHT © 1993, 1994, 1995, 1996, 2000, 2001, 2002.
USED BY PERMISSION OF NAVPRESS PUBLISHING GROUP.

PUBLISHED BY BARBOUR PUBLISHING, INC., P.O. BOX 719,
UHRICHSVILLE, OHIO 44683, www.barbourpublishing.com

ecpa Member of the
Evangelical Christian
Publishers Association

PRINTED IN CHINA.

Crazy About My Dog

ALL THINGS BRIGHT AND BEAUTIFUL,
ALL CREATURES GREAT AND SMALL,
ALL THINGS WISE AND WONDERFUL,
THE LORD GOD MADE THEM ALL.
~Cecil Frances Alexander

I'M CRAZY ABOUT MY DOG
BECAUSE HE IS A FEARLESS
PROTECTOR OF OUR HOME.

I'M CRAZY ABOUT MY DOG
BECAUSE SHE HELPS ME
STAY IN SHAPE.

I'M CRAZY ABOUT MY DOG
BECAUSE HE IS ALWAYS PREPARED
FOR A NICE LONG WALK.

I'M CRAZY ABOUT MY DOG
BECAUSE SHE CHEERS ME UP
WHEN I'M DISCOURAGED.

I'M CRAZY ABOUT MY DOG
BECAUSE POUND FOR POUND HE IS
ONE TOUGH CUSTOMER.

I'M CRAZY ABOUT MY DOG
BECAUSE NO MATTER HOW TOUGH
MY DAY HAS BEEN,
SHE'S ALWAYS HAPPY TO SEE ME.

I'M CRAZY ABOUT MY DOG BECAUSE
HE IS WELL MANNERED AND KNOWS
HIS PLACE IN OUR HOME.

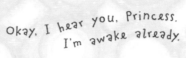

I'M CRAZY ABOUT MY DOG
BECAUSE SHE MAKES SURE I DON'T
OVERSLEEP IN THE MORNING.

I'M CRAZY ABOUT MY DOG
BECAUSE HE IS SMART ENOUGH
TO COMMUNICATE WHAT HE NEEDS.

Twinkie...not my azaleas!

I'M CRAZY ABOUT MY DOG
BECAUSE SHE'S ALWAYS READY
TO HELP WITH YARD WORK.

I'M CRAZY ABOUT MY DOG
BECAUSE HE PLAYS SO NICELY
WITH THE NEIGHBOR'S CAT.

I'M CRAZY ABOUT MY DOG BECAUSE
SHE IS WONDERFUL WITH CHILDREN.

I'M CRAZY ABOUT MY DOG BECAUSE
HE KEEPS TRAFFIC MOVING SMOOTHLY
IN FRONT OF OUR HOUSE.

I'M CRAZY ABOUT MY DOG
BECAUSE OF HER STUNNING
SENSE OF FASHION.

I'M CRAZY ABOUT MY DOG
BECAUSE HE ISN'T A FINICKY EATER.

I'M CRAZY ABOUT MY DOG
BECAUSE SHE LOVES ROAD TRIPS.

I'M CRAZY ABOUT MY DOG BECAUSE
I KNOW ALL GOOD DOGS GO TO HEAVEN.

I'M CRAZY ABOUT MY DOG
BECAUSE HE REALLY GETS
INTO THE CHRISTMAS SPIRIT.

I'M CRAZY ABOUT MY DOG
BECAUSE SHE'S GOT GREAT TASTE
IN SHOES, JUST LIKE ME.

I'M CRAZY ABOUT MY DOG
BECAUSE HE LOOKS MARVELOUS
AFTER HIS BATH.

I'M CRAZY ABOUT MY DOG BECAUSE SHE'S SO THOUGHTFUL TO BRING ME PRESENTS I'M SURE TO LIKE.

I'M CRAZY ABOUT MY DOG
BECAUSE HE LIKES TO JOIN RIGHT
IN ON FAMILY GAME NIGHT.

I'M CRAZY ABOUT MY DOG BECAUSE
SHE IS VERY UNDERSTANDING WHEN
WE HAVE TO LEAVE HER HOME ALONE.

I'M CRAZY ABOUT MY DOG
BECAUSE HE KNOWS HOW
TO SLOW DOWN AND ENJOY LIFE.

I'M CRAZY ABOUT MY DOG BECAUSE
IN HIS ENTHUSIASM FOR LIFE HE
DOESN'T TAKE SHORTCUTS.

I'M CRAZY ABOUT MY DOG BECAUSE
SHE MAKES FRIENDS SO EASILY.

I'M CRAZY ABOUT MY DOG BECAUSE
HE HAS A BEAUTIFUL SINGING VOICE.

I'M CRAZY ABOUT MY DOG
BECAUSE SHE KNOWS HOW TO
MAKE GUESTS FEEL WELCOME.

I'M CRAZY ABOUT MY DOG
BECAUSE FRANKLY, I THINK
HE'S A HANDSOME LITTLE RASCAL.

I'M CRAZY ABOUT MY DOG BECAUSE
SHE'S ABSOLUTELY CRAZY ABOUT ME.

I'M CRAZY ABOUT MY DOG
BECAUSE I KNEW HE WAS MINE FROM
THE FIRST SECOND I SAW HIM.

I'M CRAZY ABOUT MY DOG BECAUSE SHE
REALLY IS A MEMBER OF THE FAMILY.

I'M CRAZY ABOUT MY DOG BECAUSE
HE HELPS CLEAN UP AFTER DINNER.

I'M CRAZY ABOUT MY DOG
BECAUSE SHE IS A GREAT LISTENER
AND NEVER GOSSIPS.

I'M CRAZY ABOUT MY DOG BECAUSE
HE SEEMS TO REALLY UNDERSTAND
WHAT THE TV SHOWS ARE ABOUT.

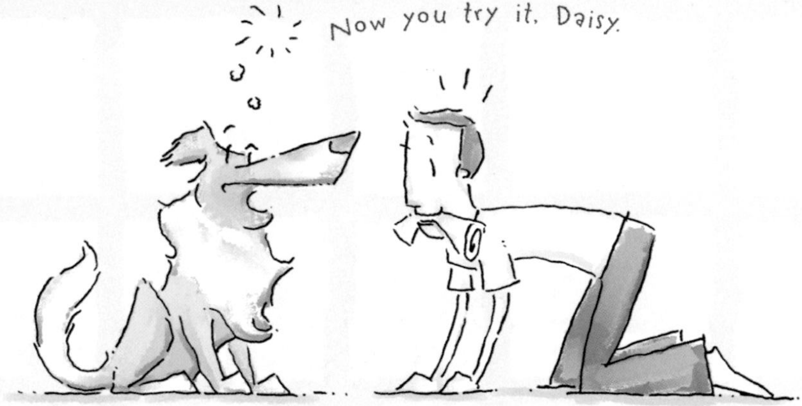
Now you try it, Daisy.

I'M CRAZY ABOUT MY DOG BECAUSE
SHE IS SO SMART IT'S EASY
TO TEACH HER TRICKS.

I'M CRAZY ABOUT MY DOG BECAUSE
HE LIKES TO SPEND TIME WITH MY
DAUGHTER AND HER NEW BOYFRIEND.

I'M CRAZY ABOUT MY DOG
BECAUSE SHE SEEMS JUST LIKE
ONE OF THE KIDS.

I'M CRAZY ABOUT MY DOG BECAUSE
HE IS EASYGOING AND COOPERATIVE.

(USUALLY.)

Rex, come back right no-o-o-o-o-w!
SCHOOL of OBEDIENCE
SCHOOL of OBEDIENCE

I'M CRAZY ABOUT MY DOG BECAUSE
HE PASSED OBEDIENCE SCHOOL
WITH FLYING COLORS.

I'M CRAZY ABOUT MY DOG BECAUSE
SHE MAKES ME FEEL SAFE AT NIGHT.

I'M CRAZY ABOUT MY DOG
BECAUSE, EVEN IF HE ROAMS,
HE ALWAYS FINDS HIS WAY HOME.

I'M CRAZY ABOUT MY DOG
BECAUSE SHE'S ALWAYS
HAPPY TO BE WITH ME.

(AND SHE'S NEVER JUDGMENTAL, EVEN
WHEN I'M IN A BIT OF A BAD MOOD.)

I'M CRAZY ABOUT MY DOG BECAUSE
HE REMINDS ME TO SLOW DOWN AND
SAVOR GOD'S WONDERFUL CREATION.

I'M CRAZY ABOUT MY DOG
BECAUSE SHE TRULY IS THE
GR-R-R-R-R-EATEST FRIEND!

I'M CRAZY ABOUT MY DOG BECAUSE
HE WAS CREATED BY A GOD WHO THINKS
DOGS ARE GREAT!

GOD LOOKED
OVER EVERYTHING
HE HAD MADE;
IT WAS SO GOOD,
SO VERY GOOD!

GENESIS 1:31